DEINOCHEIRUS

and Other Big, Fierce Dinosaurs

by Dougal Dixon

illustrated by
Steve Weston and James Field

PICTURE WINDOW BOOKS
Minneapolis, Minnesota

Picture Window Books
5115 Excelsior Boulevard
Suite 232
Minneapolis, MN 55416
877-845-8392
www.picturewindowbooks.com

Printed in the United States of America.

Library of Congress Cataloging-in-Publication Data
Dixon, Dougal.
Deinocheirus and other big, fierce dinosaurs / by
Dougal Dixon ; illustrated by Steve Weston &
James Field.
p. cm. — (Dinosaur find)
Includes index.
ISBN 978-1-4048-4015-7 (library binding)
1. Deinocheirus—Juvenile literature. 2. Dinosaurs—
Juvenile literature. I. Weston, Steve, ill. II. Field,
James, ill. III. Title.
QE862.S3D5934 2008
567.912—dc22   2007040924

Acknowledgments
This book was produced for Picture Window Books
by Bender Richardson White, U.K.

Illustrations by James Field (cover and pages 4–5, 9,
13, 17, 21) and Steve Weston (pages 7, 11, 15, 19).
Diagrams by Stefan Chabluk.

Photographs: istockphotos pages 6 (Chrisds), 8
(Rob Zeiler), 16 (Peter Miller), 18 (Ferenc Cegledi);
bigstock photos 10 (Luis Cesar), 20 (Timothy
Lubcke); Digital Vision 14; Frank Lane Photo Agency
12 (Albert Visage).

Consultant: John Stidworthy, Scientific Fellow of
the Zoological Society, London, and former
Lecturer in the Education Department, Natural
History Museum, London.

Types of dinosaurs

In this book, a red shape at the
top of a left-hand page shows
the animal was a meat-eater.
A green shape shows it was
a plant-eater.

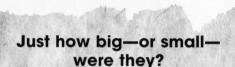

Just how big—or small—were they?

Dinosaurs were many different
sizes. We have compared their
size to one of the following:

Chicken
2 feet (60 centimeters) tall
Weight 6 pounds (2.7 kilograms)

Adult person
6 feet (1.8 meters) tall
Weight 170 pounds (76.5 kg)

Elephant
10 feet (3 m) tall
Weight 12,000 pounds
(5,400 kg)

TABLE OF CONTENTS

WHAT'S INSIDE?

Big, fierce dinosaurs! These animals lived in many places in the prehistoric world. Find out how they survived millions of years ago and what they have in common with today's animals.

BIG, FIERCE DINOSAURS

Dinosaurs lived between 230 million and 65 million years ago. There were many different kinds of dinosaurs. Some of them were big and very fierce. The fiercest dinosaurs were meat-eaters, such as *Allosaurus* and *Tyrannosaurus*. They were hunters with sharp teeth and claws. They attacked and killed other dinosaurs.

The most terrifying sight for most dinosaurs was a hungry *Tyrannosaurus* with two things on its mind—to kill and eat!

ALLOSAURUS

Pronunciation:
AL-lo-SAW-rus

Allosaurus was a big meat-eating dinosaur. Long before *Tyrannosaurus* was around, *Allosaurus* ruled the plains of what is now North America. *Allosaurus* was a deadly hunter, feeding on the big, long-necked plant-eaters of the time. It may have hunted on its own and in packs with other *Allosaurus.*

Big hunter today

The tiger is one of the fiercest of today's hunters. Like *Allosaurus* once did, the tiger preys on the smallest and weakest animals.

Size Comparison

An *Allosaurus* followed an *Apatosaurus* herd. When it spotted a weak or young animal, it quickly attacked.

DEINOCHEIRUS

Pronunciation:
dy-no-KY-rus

Deinocheirus was a big dinosaur with very long claws. Each of its claws was 10 inches (25 centimeters) long. The dinosaur could have used its claws to defend itself from attack. Some people think *Deinocheirus* might have climbed trees, using the claws to hold on to branches.

Big claws today

The modern grizzly bear can be a fierce animal. Like *Deinocheirus* once did, the grizzly bear can kill with its big claws.

Size Comparison

Deinocheirus may have used its claws to attack enemies.

SPINOSAURUS

Pronunciation:
SPY-nuh-SAW-rus

Spinosaurus was a fish-eating dinosaur that lived in what is now Africa. On its back was a huge "sail" made of skin. The sail probably soaked up heat from the sun, keeping *Spinosaurus* warm. The dinosaur had long jaws packed with sharp teeth and long claws on its fingers.

Sails today

The modern basilisk lizard has fins and a sail on its back, like *Spinosaurus* once had.

Size Comparison

Standing in the early morning sun, *Spinosaurus* waited for its body to warm up. Then the day's hunt could begin.

GIGANOTOSAURUS

Pronunciation:
gig-an-O-toe-SAW-rus

Giganotosaurus was a giant meat-eater. The dinosaur was strong and probably fought others of its own kind. For example, when a *Giganotosaurus* made a kill, other dinosaurs may have tried to steal the meal. This would have led to a fight between the dinosaurs.

Rivalry today

Lions today fight over feeding order, just as *Giganotosaurus* may have done.

Size Comparison

Once a *Giganotosaurus* killed its prey, the dinosaur had to guard the meal from other hungry dinosaurs.

CARNOTAURUS

Pronunciation:
CAR-nuh-TOR-rus

Carnotaurus was a big meat-eating dinosaur with weak arms and hands. If the animal got into a fight, it would have used teeth rather than claws to attack. A pair of horns over its eyes made *Carnotaurus* look fierce.

The face of today's hunter

The modern horned owl is a good hunter. Tufts of feathers above its eyes make it look even fiercer, just like *Carnotaurus'* horns once did.

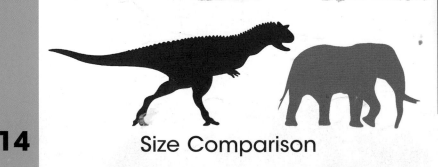

Size Comparison

Carnotaurus used sharp teeth to bite and kill its prey.

Tyrannosaurus

Pronunciation:
tie-RAN-uh-SAW-rus

Tyrannosaurus was not the biggest meat-eater to have roamed the Earth, but it was one of the fiercest. The dinosaur's big teeth could slice through skin and bone. Sometimes it killed prey. At other times, it found and ate dead animals.

Scavengers today

Like *Tyrannosaurus* once did, modern hyenas hunt down and kill prey. But more often, the hyenas search for dead animals they can eat.

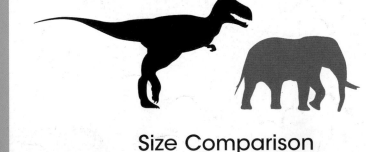

Size Comparison

Looking out for other scavengers, *Tyrannosaurus* would feed on the rotting body of a dead dinosaur.

RUGOPS

Pronunciation:
ROO-gops

Rugops had a brightly colored, wrinkled face. The colors may have been used to communicate with other *Rugops*. But the colors also served as a warning to other animals, signaling to them that *Rugops* was a fierce dinosaur.

Wrinkly face today

The modern mandrill is a kind of baboon that lives in Africa. It has a brightly colored, wrinkled face, just like *Rugops* once did.

Size Comparison

18

With its brightly colored face and strange wrinkles, *Rugops* let other animals know it was near.

Cryolophosaurus

After a meat-eating dinosaur such as *Cryolophosaurus* killed its prey, the animal ate as much as it could. The dinosaur did this because it did not know when the next meal would come along. After eating, *Cryolophosaurus* rested and disgested the food.

Big meals today

The modern python kills large animals and swallows them whole. As *Cryolophosaurus* once did, the python may have to wait awhile for its next meal.

Size Comparison

After a big meal, *Cryolophosaurus* rested while its body digested its food.

WHERE DID THEY GO?

Dinosaurs are extinct, which means that none of them are alive today. Scientists study rocks and fossils to find clues about what happened to dinosaurs.

People have different explanations about what happened. Some people think a huge asteroid that hit Earth caused all sorts of climate changes, which caused the dinosaurs to die. Others think volcanic eruptions caused the climate change and that killed the dinosaurs. No one knows for sure what happened to all of the dinosaurs.

Glossary

claws—tough, usually curved fingernails or toenails

digested—when food is broken down inside the body

herd—a large group of animals that moves, feeds, and sleeps together

horns—hard, pointed structures on the head

prey—animals hunted for food by meat-eaters

sail—tall, thin, upright structure on the back of some animals

scavenger—an animal that feeds on the bodies of animals that are already dead

signal—to make a sign, warning, or hint

To Learn More

More Books to Read

Clark, Neil, and William Lindsay. *1001 Facts About Dinosaurs.* New York: Dorling Kindersley, 2002.

Dixon, Dougal. *Dougal Dixon's Amazing Dinosaurs.* Honesdale, Penn.: Boyds Mills Press, 2007.

Holtz, Thomas R., and Michael Brett-Surman. *Jurassic Park Institute Dinosaur Field Guide.* New York: Random House, 2001.

On the Web

FactHound offers a safe, fun way to find Web sites related to topics in this book. All of the sites on FactHound have been researched by our staff.

1. Visit *www.facthound.com*

2. Type in this special code:140484015X

3. Click on the FETCH IT button.

Your trusty FactHound will fetch the best Web sites for you!

Index

Look for all of the books in the Dinosaur Find series: